60

FARRAR
STRAUS
GIROUX

Doug Macomber

CARL PHILLIPS, *Quiver of Arrows: Selected Poems, 1986–2006*

Carl Phillips is the author of eight books of poetry, including *Riding Westward*; *The Rest of Love*, a finalist for the National Book Award; and *The Tether*, which won the Kingsley Tufts Poetry Award. His other books include a translation of Sophocles' *Philoctetes* and *Coin of the Realm: Essays on the Life and Art of Poetry*. Phillips's many honors include the Theodore Roethke Foundation Memorial Prize, the Thom Gunn Award for Gay Male Poetry, an Award in Literature from the American Academy of Arts and Letters, fellowships from the Guggenheim Foundation and the Library of Congress, and, in 2006, the Academy of American Poets Fellowship, given in memory of James Ingram Merrill, for distinguished poetic achievement at mid-career. He teaches at Washington University in St. Louis.

Quiver of Arrows

SELECTED POEMS, 1986–2006

Dwayne, Dwayne —

Quiver of Arrows

stay wild, but

SELECTED POEMS, 1986–2006

stay on the path

Carl Phillips

of words —

FARRAR STRAUS GIROUX, NEW YORK

Carl Phillips

_CC 2007._

FARRAR, STRAUS AND GIROUX
19 Union Square West, New York 10003

Distributed in Canada by Douglas & McIntyre Ltd.
Printed in the United States of America
First edition, 2007

Grateful acknowledgment is made for permission to reprint the following poems:
"X," "Passing," "Life Lessons from Art," "With Love for the Night Patrol,"
"Leda, After the Swan," "The Glade," "Fra Lippo Lippi and the Vision of Henley,"
"Death of the Sibyl," and "Blue" from *In the Blood*, copyright © 1992
by Carl Phillips. Reprinted by permission of University Press of New England,
Hanover, NH. "The Compass," "King of Hearts," "Cotillion," "Cortège," "Youth with
Satyr, Both Resting," "Glads," "A Mathematics of Breathing," and "What Myth Is" from
Cortège, copyright © 1995 by Carl Phillips. Reprinted by permission of
Graywolf Press. "The Trees," "Alba: Innocence," "No Kingdom," "Alba: Failure,"
"A Great Noise," "Tunnel," "As from a Quiver of Arrows," "Meditation," and "From
the Devotions" from *From the Devotions*, copyright © 1998 by Carl Phillips.
Reprinted by permission of Graywolf Press. "A Kind of Meadow," "Parable,"
" 'All art . . . ,' " "Hymn," "The Gods Leaving," "Against His Quitting the Torn Field,"
"Would-Be Everlasting," "Retreat," "The Truth," and "The Kill" from *Pastoral*,
copyright © 2000 by Carl Phillips. Reprinted by permission of Graywolf Press.

Library of Congress Cataloging-in-Publication Data
Phillips, Carl, 1959–
    Quiver of arrows : selected poems, 1986–2006 /
Carl Phillips.— 1st ed.
        p.   cm.
    ISBN-13: 978-0-374-53078-5 (pbk. : alk. paper)
    ISBN-10: 0-374-53078-5 (pbk. : alk. paper)
    I. Title.

PS3566.H476 Q58 2007
811'.54—dc22

                                        2006029981

www.fsgbooks.com

1   3   5   7   9   10   8   6   4   2

CONTENTS

FROM *In the Blood* (1992)

X 3

Passing 5

Life Lessons from Art 7

With Love for the Night Patrol 9

Leda, After the Swan 11

The Glade 13

Fra Lippo Lippi and the Vision of Henley 15

Death of the Sibyl 16

Blue 18

FROM *Cortège* (1995)

The Compass 23

King of Hearts 25

Cotillion 27

Cortège 29

Youth with Satyr, Both Resting 38

Glads 40

A Mathematics of Breathing 42

What Myth Is 45

FROM *From the Devotions* (1998)

The Trees 49

Alba: Innocence 51

No Kingdom 53

Alba: Failure 55

A Great Noise 57

Tunnel 60

As from a Quiver of Arrows 63

Meditation 65

From the Devotions 72

FROM *Pastoral* (2000)

A Kind of Meadow 77

Parable 80

"All art . . ." 82

Hymn 84

The Gods Leaving 86

Against His Quitting the Torn Field 88

Would-Be Everlasting 91

Retreat 93

The Truth 95

The Kill 99

FROM *The Tether* (2001)

Luck 103

Spoils, Dividing 105

The Point of the Lambs 107

Roman Glass 110

Stagger 112

Regalia Figure 114

Lustrum 117

Tether 120

Caravan 123

The Figure, the Boundary, the Light 125

Revision 127

FROM *Rock Harbor* (2002)

Golden 133

As a Blow, from the West 135

The Clearing 140

By Hard Stages 143

The Clarity 146

To Break, to Ride 148

Trade 151

Return to the Land of the Golden Apples 153

Fretwork 155

Halo 157

FROM *The Rest of Love* (2004)

Custom 163

Singing 164

Vow 165

Like Stitches Where the Moths
Have Made an Opening 167

Late Apollo 168

All It Takes 171

White Dog 172

Fervor 173

Fresco: Cove and Spur 175

If a Wilderness 178

Here, on Earth 179

Like Cuttings for a Wreath
of Praise and Ransom 182

Fray 183

FROM *Riding Westward* (2006)

Bright World 187

Radiance versus Ordinary Light 188

Ocean 189

Brocade 190

Island 193

Bow Down 194

After 198

To a Legend 199

The Messenger 201

Forecast 202

Translation 203

Break of Day 204

Riding Westward 206

In the Blood

(1992)

X

Several hours past that
of knife and fork

laid across one another
to say done, X

is still for the loose
stitch of beginners,

the newlywed
grinding next door

that says no one
but you, the pucker

of lips only, not yet
the wounds those lips

may be drawn to. X,
as in variable,

anyone's body, any set
of conditions, your

body scaling whatever
fence of chain-metal Xs

desire throws up, what
your spreadeagled limbs

suggest, falling, and
now, after. X, not

just for where in my
life you've landed,

but here too, where
your ass begins its

half-shy, half-weary
dividing, where I

sometimes lay my head
like a flower, and

think I mean something
by it. X is all I keep

meaning to cross out.

Passing

When the Famous Black Poet speaks,
I understand

that his is the same unnervingly slow
rambling method of getting from A to B
that I hated in my father,
my father who always told me
don't shuffle.

The Famous Black Poet is
speaking of the dark river in the mind
that runs thick with the heroes of color,
Jackie R., Bessie, Billie, Mr. Paige, anyone
who knew how to sing or when to run.
I think of my grandmother, said
to have dropped dead from the evil eye,
of my lesbian aunt who saw cancer and
a generally difficult future headed her way
in the still water
of her brother's commode.
I think of voodoo in the bottoms of soup-cans,
and I want to tell the poet that the blues
is *not* my name, that Alabama
is something I cannot use
in my business.

He is so like my father,
I don't ask the Famous Black Poet,
afterwards,
to remove his shoes,
knowing the inexplicable black
and pink I will find there, a cut
gone wrong in five places.
I don't ask him to remove
his pants, since that too
is known, what has never known
a blade, all the spaces between,
where we differ . . .

I have spent years tugging
between my legs,
and proved nothing, really.
I wake to the sheets I kicked aside,
and examine where they've failed to mend
their own creases, resembling some silken
obstruction, something pulled
from my father's chest, a bad heart,
a lung,

the lung of the Famous Black Poet
saying nothing I want to understand.

Life Lessons from Art

FOR EVY

Leave every room its share
of dark corners,
its shelves of relics,
or replicas of same,
to cast additional shadow;
always, the flesh—be it

the girl-student's lifted
arm, the bit of neck escaping
from the meister's lace cravat—

should be the primary source of light:

if there are windows,
they are only to show some emblem
of the world you have chosen
largely to ignore, a plow, or a ship
with sails folded, griffins rising where
the eye of the cartographer fails,
skies doubling as the pasty brow of God.

As appropriate, paint yourself
into the grain of a half-eaten slice of orange,
the cameo holding the infant's
baptismal gown together,

include your reflection
in the doorknob, the porcelain
sconce, the tea-service the newly
married couple has already forgotten,

anywhere they'll think to look last.
With these exceptions, leave the bulk
of your work unsigned.

With Love for the Night Patrol

After the echoes unwrap about us,
the world is unchanged: trees broken and prone
like cool stigmatics, bit of bird in the bush,
wagerable sounds. There is rain, and
the same doubt I couple with the breaking
of dangerous habits. It is difficult
to know what to walk away from.

We tramp through loosely stitched, folding miles
of field whose pattern eludes us. A child's gown
clings to the spokes of an abandoned wheel,
maybe there were houses here.
Every shift of light rears and tips
toward instruction, a clue, the way
things do at home, in a faucet's spit
and cock, in the flight
of a knife.
We push our eyes absently at shadow,
and move on, feeling ready for very little.

I've seen the moon bruise a good jaw down
to pearl, as if scrubbed by rough cloth,
or the fine dirt in the air.
I have marked how the body's action loses
its signature in crisis, frames pitched and
wilting in unison, how legs and arms
dumbly flutter like spent occasions

into the wind.
Mostly,
I think of those many-sectioned dreams in which
night is figured with bodiless advice, missed entries,
deaths that are none of the several small ones

you've come to expect, and you resign yourself
to your own dead weight, when ascending is
the only right move and you know it, you know

you're in the part nobody reads.

Leda, After the Swan

Perhaps,
in the exaggerated grace
of his weight
settling,

the wings
raised, held in
strike-or-embrace
position,

I recognized
something more
than swan, I can't say.

There was just
this barely defined
shoulder, whose feathers
came away in my hands,

and the bit of world
left beyond it, coming down

to the heat-crippled field,

ravens the precise color of
sorrow in good light, neither
black nor blue, like fallen
stitches upon it,

and the hour forever,
it seemed, half-stepping
its way elsewhere—

then
everything, I
remember, began
happening more quickly.

The Glade

Here, complete with half-swallowed cry
of small game rising, stirring
the light, is that ease

with which a legend goes
languorously down on itself,
slow-dying;

this is the air left behind, thick
with the whir of bees flagging, smell
of meadow that's spent all its arrows,

where every dream is
of difficult breathing, of desire
as a finally grounded bird

whose limbs and blue-black wings
dangle from the dreamer's mouth,
refusing to come loose . . .

Here,
where his body lay, gather up all
the broken-stemmed flowers;

photograph the water, that in
the wind repeatedly makes for shore
and misses—

these, for dark Narcissus
who, whatever else and more
he may have been,

was never ours.

Fra Lippo Lippi and
the Vision of Henley

If, in depicting the angels, I cannot
avoid something, as well, of what
the river that day cast before me,

the musculature of the rowers' arms,
together streaking the air of those
otherwise empty, unremarkable hours;

if only now, after the mechanical
drown   recover   drown of the oars in
their hands, do I understand wings

and the scaled-down pattern for
suffering that every wing, surely,
is lined with, do, Monsignor,

forgive me. By your grace, again,
this is what happened: at first,
only the heat, the cool water . . .

Death of the Sibyl

The world, when it comes, is not the fist
and palm of a lover's roulette, nothing
to brace for. There are no visions.

The blue stops here, as the walls do,
light spills with the candor of money
or jangled music on the morning's disorder:

the knife, streaked and at rest, spent
fruit, plates round and flat as an old,
unquestioned routine. Outside, the hours

drift and pick at the air, as if coming
and going were grave decisions, as if there
were still an immediacy, somewhere, to

things as they are. You know better.
Your body isn't the restive field it was,
clouds share none of the marbled indifference

of statues, whose absent limbs and dark-socketed
heads once triggered desire. Surely this
is the backside of God, to lie down

in a room of no accidents, touch your own
flesh or not, to nobody's direction, grip
sheets in your mouth and know passion is

little more than a wound to be straddled,
shadow something less than pearls in
retreat. To feel empty as seed to fire,

hear the rush of whole lives passing
elsewhere, without you, and still believe
you have not been entirely abandoned.

Blue

As through marble or the lining of
certain fish split open and scooped
clean, this is the blue vein
that rides, where the flesh is even
whiter than the rest of her, the splayed
thighs mother forgets, busy struggling
for command over bones: her own,
those of the chaise longue, all
equally uncooperative, and there's
the wind, too. This is her hair, gone
from white to blue in the air.

This is the black, shot with blue, of my dark
daddy's knuckles, that do not change, ever.
Which is to say they are no more pale
in anger than at rest, or when, as
I imagine them now, they follow
the same two fingers he has always used
to make the rim of every empty blue
glass in the house sing.
Always, the same
blue-to-black sorrow
no black surface can entirely hide.

Under the night, somewhere
between the white that is nothing so much as
blue, and the black that is, finally, nothing,

I am the man neither of you remembers.
Shielding, in the half-dark,
the blue eyes I sometimes forget
I don't have. Pulling my own stoop-
shouldered kind of blues across paper.
Apparently misinformed about the rumored
stuff of dreams: everywhere I inquired,
I was told look for blue.

Cortège

(1995)

The Compass

a star

dog with torch in its mouth

a finger-ring   but no finger
broken cup   what is lonely
the single breast the beehive resembles
a pair of breasts on a dish

what else
comes in pairs   tongs   forceps
a key crossing a key
the cross but   recumbent or

knocked over
what is called the cross saltire
t
turned on its side

x
that one and
that one and
what stands for

gridiron for the having been roasted alive
a ship's windlass for around
what the intestine   pulled out into
the salt air   was bound fast

what flies   a raven
a winged lion
a winged ox
a man   but with wings

an arrow

what is lovely   an arrow

King of Hearts

Somewhere now, someone is missing him,
since here he is for the taking, nicked
at three of his four corners, decked out

in the fade of much play, his two heads
laid prone on the sidewalk before you.

Like you, in this heat and humidity, no
wind, when it comes, moves him. Like you,

he knows a thing, maybe, about wilting—
how, like sleep or some particularly

miserable defeat played over but this time
in slow motion, it has its own fine beauty.

■

Tonight,
          once you've found him, when you've

brought him home, the man with a face as
close as you'll ever get to the other one,

the one it was easy enough, earlier, not to
pick up, to step on, even, and move slowly

but unbothered away from, you'll only remember

the part about wilting.
                    And even that, as

you lift his ass toward you, as your hands
spread it open until it resembles nothing

so much as a raw heart but with a seemingly
endless hole through it—even that will

fade.
          Him, between drink and the good money

you've paid, doing whatever you tell him.
Him throwing back whatever words you hand out.

You're the king, you're the king, him saying.

Cotillion

Every one of these bodies, those in drag, those
not, loves a party, that much is clear. The blonde
with the amazing lashes—lashes, more amazingly,

his own—tells me it is like when a small bird
rises, sometimes, like the difficult thing is not to.
I think he is talking about joy or pain or desire

or any of the several things desire, sweet drug,
too sweet, can lead to. I think he means moments,
like this one, sudden, when in no time I know that

these lashes, the mouth that could use now more
painting, these hairless, shaven-for-the-event arms
whose skin, against the shine of the gown, a spill of

blood and sequins the arms themselves spill from,
glitters still, but dully, like what is not the
main prize does always—I know this man is mine,

if I want him. Meanwhile around us, the room fairly
staggers with men, and an aching to be lovely—loved,
even. As in any crowd, lately, of people, the heavy

corsage of them stepping in groups, the torn bloom
that is each taking his own particular distance,
I think the trick is one neither of joining or not

joining, but of holding, as long as I can, to some
space between, call it rest for the wary, the slow
dragging to nowhere I call heaven. I'm dancing

maybe, but not on air: this time through water.

Cortège

Do not imagine you can abdicate. AUDEN

PROLOGUE

If the sea could dream, and if the sea
were dreaming now, the dream
would be the usual one: Of the Flesh.
The letter written in the dream would go
something like: *Forgive me—love, Blue.*

I. THE VIEWING (A CHORUS)

O what, then, did he look like?

He had a good body.

And how came you to know this?

His body was naked.

Say the sound of his body.

His body was quiet.

Say again—quiet?

He was sleeping.

You are sure of this? Sleeping?

Inside it, yes. Inside it.

II. PAVILION

Sometimes, a breeze: a canvas
flap will rise and, inside,
someone stirs; *a bird? a flower?*

One is thinking *Should there be*
thirst, I have only to reach
for the swollen bag of skin

beside me, I have only to touch
my mouth that is meant for a flower
to it, and drink.

One is for now certain he is
one of those poems that stop only;
they do not end.

One says without actually saying it
I am sometimes a book of such poems,
I am other times a flower and lovely

pressed like so among them, but
always they forget me.
I miss my name.

They are all of them heat-
weary, anxious for evening as for
some beautiful to the bone

messenger to come. They will open
again for him. His hands are good.
His message is a flower.

III. THE TASTING (A CHORUS)

O what, then, did he taste like?

He tasted of sorrow.

And how came you to know this?

My tongue still remembers.

Say the taste that is sorrow.

Game, fallen unfairly.

And yet, you still tasted?

Still, I tasted.

Did you say to him something?

I could not speak, for hunger.

IV. INTERIOR

And now,
the candle blooms gorgeously away
from his hand—

and the light has made
blameless all over
the body of him (mystery,

mystery), twelvefold
shining, by grace of twelve
mirrors the moth can't stop

attending. Singly, in no order,
it flutters against, beats
the glass of each one,

as someone elsewhere
is maybe beating upon
a strange door now,

somebody knocks
and knocks at a new
country, of which

nothing is understood—
no danger occurs
to him, though

danger could be any
of the unusually wild
flowers

that, either side of the road,
spring.
When he slows, bends down and

closer, to see or
to take one—it is as if
he knows something to tell it.

V. THE DREAMING (A CHORUS)

O what, then, did it feel like?
>> I dreamed of an arrow.

And how came you to know him?
>> I dreamed he was wanting.

Say the dream of him wanting.
>> A swan, a wing folding.

Why do you weep now?
>> I remember.

Tell what else you remember.
>> The swan was mutilated.

ENVOI

And I came to where was nothing but drowning
and more drowning, and saw to where the sea—
besides flesh—was, as well, littered with boats,
how each was blue but trimmed with white, to each
a name I didn't know and then, recalling,
did. And ignoring the flesh that, burning, gives
more stink than heat, I dragged what boats I could
to the shore and piled them severally in a tree-
less space, and lit a fire that didn't take
at first—the wood was wet—and then, helped by
the wind, became a blaze so high the sea
itself, along with the bodies in it, seemed
to burn. I watched as each boat fell to flame:
Vincent and *Matthew* and, last, what bore your name.

Youth with Satyr, Both Resting

There are certain words—*ecstasy*, *abandon*,
surrender—we can wait all our lives,
sometimes,

not so much to use
as to use correctly;
then the moment at last comes,

the right scene but more impossibly
different than any we'd earlier imagined,
and we stumble, catching

instead at nouns like *desire*, that
could as easily be verbs,
unstable adjectives like *rapt* or *unseemly*.

We find that for once nothing at hand
serves quite as well as the finger doing
what it does, pointing:

at the wine whose slim remains
the two glasses—tipped slightly, given
over to the grass as to their own sweet brand

of longing—look like any moment
letting go of;
or the boy's hand, fallen in such a way as

to just miss
touching the predictably stiff phallus—no
other word here will do—of the satyr;

or at how the O of the boy's mouth,
barely open,
is the same O that the satyr's beard, abruptly

arching away from his shag-covered chest, and
on, skyward,
seems most like wanting to curl into, if only

it could . . . which in turn is
the same O repeated by those the grapes'
twisting vines—too artificially, perhaps—

string above and,
to either side of the two sleepers,
in the manner of any number of unresolvable

themes, let dangle.

Glads

Three, at the most four days later,
they're dying, knuckled
over at whichever flower has bloomed

largest. The way everything beautiful
finally breaks because of, from it.
As if this were necessary. The reason,

maybe, why the loveliest things are always
also the most ruined:
a man's aging breast falling until,

naturally, brassieres come to mind;
or why, given any crumbled wall, nobody
thinks to ask where did they go to,

bring them back, all those
missing pieces.
The difference between a cock at plain

rest, for once longing to put itself
nowhere special,
and one that, just done thirsting,

collapses, curls slowly back in on
itself.
In Renaissance Italy,

when depicting the saints and Christ
in mid-torment was all the rage,
the painters chose for their backdrops

the most unremarkable buildings,
landscapes stranded in neutral, people
doing the dull things they still do—

plowing, benchwarming a small hill,
idly swinging a staff at livestock,
or at nothing, gone fishing.

The idea was to throw up into relief,
in its rawest form, sheer affliction.
The motto was

No distractions from suffering, hence
the skies: in general, clear
or just clearing, washed of anything

like rescue birds hope clouds mercy.

A Mathematics of Breathing

Think of any of several arched
colonnades to a cathedral,

how the arches
like fountains, say,

or certain limits in calculus,
when put to the graph paper's crosstrees,

never quite meet any promised heaven,
instead at their vaulted heights

falling down to the abruptly ending
base of the next column,

smaller, the one smaller
past that, at last

dying, what is
called perspective.

This is the way buildings do it.

II.

You have seen them, surely, busy paring
the world down to what it is mostly,

proverb: so many birds in a bush.
Suddenly they take off, and at first

it seems your particular hedge itself
has sighed deeply,

that the birds are what come,
though of course it is just the birds

leaving one space for others.
After they've gone, put your ear to the bush,

listen. There are three sides: the leaves'
releasing of something, your ear where it

finds it, and the air in between, to say
equals. There is maybe a fourth side,

not breathing.

III.

In *One Thousand and One Nights*,
there are only a thousand,

Scheherazade herself is the last one,
for the moment held back,

for a moment all the odds hang even.
The stories she tells she tells mostly

to win another night of watching the prince
drift into a deep sleeping beside her,

the chance to touch one more time
his limbs, going,

gone soft already with dreaming.
When she tells her own story,

Breathe in,
breathe out

is how it starts.

What Myth Is

Not only what lasts, but what
applies over time also. So
maybe, for all my believing, not

you, on either count. Anymore
than this hand where it falls,
here, on your body; or than

your body itself, however good
sometimes at making—even now,
in sleep—a point carry. Not

this morning, either, that under
the heat has already begun
failing; nor, for all their pre—

Ice Age glamour—what is
mythical, at best, not myth—
these Japanese beetles that off

and on hit the window's limp
screen, fall in, even. Who
make of the trees' leaves a

thin lace the air, like memory,
languidly fingers. Whose wings,
like yours where sometimes I

see them, flash broad, green-
gold in the sun, to say bronze.
When they fold them, it's hard

to believe they fly, ever.

From the Devotions

(1998)

The Trees

All night. From behind
curtain, turned suddenly all lifting
veil. From behind the screen behind that.

Their motion—their leaves' motion—
that of a torn wing,
that same unlovely

snagged flight, to the same half-tune
(your breathing)
to which the hours on blue

ankles parade as
down some questionable boulevard.
All night,

as if that other one (before
you, my body beside someone's but
not yet yours), when

"even the moon, even clouds"
were saying the trees that—as now,
then too—I was certain

could not know.
They think everything ends . . .
If so, then

why not this wake of losses (inevitable?
earned?)
that I have often enough come

so close to forgetting, I turn around
—and yes,
they are still with,

I think they will always be with—
no one is waving good-bye.
The trees

wave but, except to say "wind—
up again," this
means nothing. Sometimes,

we hold on to a life tightly.
Foolish; sad.
Not to know that it has already left us.

Alba: Innocence

Sunday. The bells, as expected. I cannot
help it if I rise, if finding the room too
fraught with light—all of it, the white
walls, the rinsed notion (always almost

inside then just out of reach) of God, your
body gleaming in sleep where the sun falls
on it and away from, falls on and away—
I have to shut my one good eye and at once

the leaves falling but now blurred make it
possible to see how it happens, a bruise
lifting itself over time from the darker
blues to, slowly, something like amber,

to at last whatever, before the wounding,
the flesh was. Imagining the flesh before
or without knowledge, I want to say it is
most like song untrained, whose beauty,

when it occurs, surprises even itself—
but isn't it also, more commonly, just
meat, or isn't it good soil waiting, that
does not, cannot know that it is waiting?

Therefore, it is innocence. Therefore,
a capacity for suffering more vast, even,

than the landscape whose particulars, you
remember, we drove past, the red of sunset

upon them: the bull in mid-lumbering over
the cow (still with patience, with fear?),
almost, not yet inside her; the sudden
bursting of crows, all cinders flying over

where once, presumably, was some small life.
We were tired, hungry, faintly hungry for
each other. We kept driving: east, home,
toward a dark we couldn't fast enough get to.

No Kingdom

So little wakes you—why
should a little rain,
or my leaving

to stand under it
and naked
because I can,

all neighbors down,
at last down,
for the dreaming, and

every wasp—daily, the yard's
plague—gone,
returned to

whatever shingle or board
roofs their now
thrumless heliport.

Tremblefoot,
mumbler,
you've left

your glass on the porch-railing
—neglect, as
what is fragile, seen

through,
but not at this hour empty:
the way disease does

the body, the way desire
can, or how God
is said to,

slowly rain fills the glass.
Never mind
that no kingdom was ever won

by small gestures:
I'm tipping the rainwater out.
The glass I'll put

here, where you'll find it.

Alba: Failure

If the bare trees at the glass were kings
really, I would know they bend over in grief,
mourning their lost brilliant crowns that

they can only watch, not reach as, beneath them,
they let go of all color all flash all sway,
it would be better, I wouldn't have to say *no*

they are not kings, they are trees, I know this,
and if they bend it is wind only, it is nature,
isn't it also indifference? Passing yesterday

the bodies that, wrapped and wrapped, lay
sprawled above the steam as it left the vents
of my city, I could only fumble for the words

(*dead lamb, dead lamb*) to some song to sing
parts of, I gave, but what I gave—is it
right to say it helped no one, or can I say

I brought lullaby, sealed a thin life,
awhile longer, in sleep? What is failure?
Having read how there were such things as

orchard lamps for keeping the good fruit, on
colder nights, from freezing, I was curious
for that kind of heat go the lines from

a poem I never finished. The shorter version
is: once, twice, in a difficult time, I have
failed you. No poetry corrects this. But

does it mean we don't love? In the last poem
of you waking, I am any small bird, unnoticed,
above, watching; you are the traveler who

can't know (there is fog, or no stars, a steep
dark) that the all but given up for impossible
next town is soon, soon. Come. We turn here.

A Great Noise

Then he died.
And they said: *Another soul free.*

Which was the wrong way to see it, I thought,
having been there,
having lain down beside him until

his body became rigid with what I believe
was not the stiffening of death
but of surprise, the initial
unbelief of the suddenly ex-slave hearing
Rest; let it fall now, this burden.

The proof most commonly put forth for the soul
as a thing that exists and weighs
something is that
the body weighs something less, after death—

a clean fact.

In *The Miraculous Translation of the Body
of Saint Catherine of Alexandria to Sinai,*
the number of angels required to bear the body
all that way through the air
comes to four,

which tells us nothing
about weight, or the lack of it, since
the angels depicted
are clearly those for whom

the only business is hard labor,

the work angels,
you can tell:
the musculature;
the resigned way they wear clothes.

Beyond them in rank,
in the actual presence of God,
the seraphim stand naked, ever-burning,

six-winged: two to fly with,
in back; two at the face to withstand
the impossible winds that
are God;

and a third pair—for modesty,
for the covering
of sex.

A great
noise is said to always
attend them:
less the humming of wings than
the grinding you'd expect

from the hitching of what is hot,
destructive,
and all devotion

to the highest, brightest star.

Tunnel

FOR FRANK

Come now, if ever.
When it is raining this gentle
and the first thought is of semen,
and the second thought is of lilies
when by their own pale weight
they bend, sing to the ground something,
and the third thought is of
what joy or sadness can be
available to what is finally a lily
and can't sing.

■

And you said *It is wind* and *It is heat*,
hearing the doors shift in their frames.
Because you could not say what also
to call it: God as what is relentless,
God as oil, redolent, proffered;
the final, necessary cross-stitch of
death whose meaning is that everything
finds closure; or the meaningless,
already tipped, disembodied scales
in which we are all of us, inescapably,
found wanting, because how can we
not want?

■

—In the street below, the latest version of cool need, his
   black car shining in such a way as to make all of it (that
   any children around follow, that each longs to see his own
   face given back, and the one boy, that he is chosen, is
   getting in) seem natural, inevitable.

■

the body, bright thing and holy   *the body as raft-like*

the ocean beneath it as waves   *the waves as many small fans*

the one you loved, he is dead   *the one I love, he is dead*

each wave beneath him is blue   *—blue, collapsing*

■

—Sunday morning, the Greek diner. The men in pairs from
   last night. Again the different, more difficult
   tenderness that is two men with only their briefly shared
   flesh in common as they eat and don't eat much, together.
   At the window *brush/fail, brush/fail* go the leaves.

■

After Patroklos, impatient, took the armor of Achilles,
after he put it on his own body
and rode into battle, and then died,
Achilles fell into grief—
not for the loss of the armor that was his,
but for love of the man who had last worn it,
who could never, now,
be brought back.

His goddess-mother, Thetis, hearing
as far away as the sea's floor
his uncontrollable cries, hurried to him.
A lot of words, armor, a new shield . . .

∎

Here is the sun.
Take some.
Here is the rain, in no apparent way
holy, but serving still.
Wash.
Drink.
Here is the body.
Do not imagine now balm.
The wounds are to be
left open.

As from a Quiver of Arrows

What do we do with the body, do we
burn it, do we set it in dirt or in
stone, do we wrap it in balm, honey,
oil, and then gauze and tip it onto
and trust it to a raft and to water?

What will happen to the memory of his
body, if one of us doesn't hurry now
and write it down fast? Will it be
salt or late light that it melts like?
Floss, rubber gloves, a chewed cap

to a pen elsewhere—how are we to
regard his effects, do we throw them
or use them away, do we say they are
relics and so treat them like relics?
Does his soiled linen count? If so,

would we be wrong then, to wash it?
There are no instructions whether it
should go to where are those with no
linen, or whether by night we should
memorially wear it ourselves, by day

reflect upon it folded, shelved, empty.
Here, on the floor behind his bed is
a bent photo—why? Were the two of

them lovers? Does it mean, where we
found it, that he forgot it or lost it

or intended a safekeeping? Should we
attempt to make contact? What if this
other man too is dead? Or alive, but
doesn't want to remember, is human?
Is it okay to be human, and fall away

from oblation and memory, if we forget,
and can't sometimes help it and sometimes
it is all that we want? How long, in
dawns or new cocks, does that take?
What if it is rest and nothing else that

we want? Is it a findable thing, small?
In what hole is it hidden? Is it, maybe,
a country? Will a guide be required who
will say to us how? Do we fly? Do we
swim? What will I do now, with my hands?

Meditation

THE VEIL BETWEEN

That is, they with their backs to us, they with their hands
holding nothing, no mirror to see by, no one good cure.
Us then ourselves with none of our ills in great measure
bettered—still straits desperate and perilously
narrow, births especially dubious, mice, moles, false
witness, the chills, trouble of foot, ruptures bodily and
spiritual, doubt, palpitations, storm, stiffness of neck,
of heart, overly troublesome birds in too great abundance,
death sudden or too slow, quarreling, swine both real and
only seeming to be so, bruises, losing what we want most
not to, mad dogs, luck that is bad, visual soreness, shame
and the hands—because of it—folded, likewise flood
and nowhere a raft to sail on. And they not sad, apparently,
and not particularly waving. And just the wind for a sound:
cold, hollow. Us calling it song or saying *No, it is grace.*

PERFECTION

To take everything back, reverse the limbs turned out
outrageous, the breath foundering. To wake from

where flesh—like every other road there—was
hard, lasting. And find it dream—and the dreaming,

enough. To rise full from the long table
of example: the double stags, gutted, skinned, dressed—

all that meat, at last, rendered useful;
the upturned brace of pheasant, still struggling, still

knowing dimly, more dimly, darkly the gamekeeper's
kid-hugged fist. To lie naked, down, and

squired, to either side a lord gone stiff and restive
in full court dress. To steer, on sootless,

drama-less wings those undeeded acres between seduce
and persuade. O never to get, nor have

got there. To thirst gothically, to want—
like a spire: no discernible object but more sky.

THE RIVER ROAD

That certain birds—
the eagle, in whom come together in
something like marriage rapaciousness, grace;
or, rapacious too and stuffed with grace,
all manner of falcon, also of hawk each
kind—suggested the archangels:
this makes sense.

And the sky meaning,
more nakedly than usual, only the usual
(try, you will never match it, this blue),
the river widening to reflect so much more
of the same—and weren't you hungry,
besides?—how difficult was it, just
then, to see God?

But that stretch of
flat barges on hold, each awaiting the one
sign: *Come, the water lies clear*; how, bored,
you turned away toward the chalk, no, chalk-
colored bluffs that all day had been there
but now, regarded, looked
athletic, fallen—

Confess,
it has surprised you, thus to understand the soul.

SURRENDER

As when,
into the canyon that means,
whose name—translated—
means *Without Measure, Sorrow*

from the hand that,
for so long, has meant
give,
but now—broken—gives in,

is released
the garland   /swag   /bouquet
(that—look,
look again—means

only as much as what it is:
eucalyptus,
kangaroo's paw,
the grass called eel),

that he, impossibly, might catch it.

THE DARK GROTTO

If he is disease, he is also
any wanting and more wanting
of something, he is snow. *All of these.*

Like snow, how it embraces,
becomes at first its object,
how it seems to become and
then swallows its object. *All these.*

As if the body were dependent
on outposts; and the nightwatch
—slain, asleep, drunk, or
worse, bored, unregarding: *Himself, all of these.*

Whose breast was sky-endless
and redolent of—almond?
an almond tree burning? having
already burnt, just after? *Yea, these.*

In whose lap lay the wound
not invisibly bleeding, but
the blood suggesting other
than blood: *rose, hard token, these?*

And seeing, I knew the eye:
and then I knew nothing.
And tasting, I knew the tongue:

ISAIAH

Who are these that fly   like cloud
             Enter into the rock
             and hide in the dust

             ■

An antelope in a net
The cup of staggering
             Is there not a lie in my right hand

             ■

The timbrel   breathless   falls toward song
             We moan and moan
             like doves

             ■

The oil of gladness instead
             of mourning
The mantle of praise instead of   a faint spirit

             ■

> Go
and fall backward
All flesh is grass   The grass withers

                    ∎

The grass
shall become reeds
            And be broken   And rushes   And snared

From the Devotions

I.

As if somewhere, away, a door had slammed shut.
—But not metal; not wood.

Or as when something is later remembered only
as something dark in the dream:

torn, bruised, dream-slow
descending, it could be anything—

tiling, clouds,
you again, beautifully consistent, in no

usual or masterable way   *leaves, a woman's*
shaken-loose throat, shattered

eyes of the seer, palms, ashes, the flesh
instructing; you, silent.

A sky, a sea requires crossing and, like that,
there is a boat or, like that, a plane:

for whom is it this way now, when
as if still did I lie down beside, still

turn to, touch
                    I can't, I could not save you?

II.

Not, despite what you believed, that
all travel necessarily ends here, at the sea.

I am back, but only because.
As the sun only happens to meet the water

in such a way that the water becomes
a kind of cuirass: how each piece takes

and, for nothing, gives back whatever light—
sun's, moon's. A bird that is not a gull

passes over; I mark what you would: underneath,
at the tip of either wing, a fluorescent-white

moon, or round star. Does the bird itself
ever see this? According to you   *many have*

had the ashes of lovers strewn here,
on this beach   on this water that now beats at,

now seems to want just to rest alongside.
The dead can't know we miss them   Presumably

we were walking   *that we are walking*
upon them.

III.

All night, again,
a wind that failed to bring storm—

instead, the Paradise dream: the abandoned
one nest at a bad angle—in danger,

and what it is to not know it;
the equally abandoned one tree that,

for the time being, holds it—alone,
and what it is to not know it.

All morning, it has been the fog
thinning at last,

as if that were the prayer,
the streets filling with men   *as if they*

were divine answer and not just
what happens. Do I love less, if less is

all I remember? Your mouth, like a hole
to fly through. What you understood

of the flesh: how always first are we
struck down.   *Then we rise; are astounded.*

FROM

Pastoral

(2000)

A Kind of Meadow

—shored
by trees at its far ending,
as is the way in moral tales:

whether trees as trees actually,
for their shadow and what
inside of it

hides, threatens, calls to;
or as ever-wavering conscience,
cloaked now, and called Chorus;

or, between these, whatever
falls upon the rippling and measurable,
but none to measure it, thin

fabric of *this stands for.*
A kind of meadow, and then
trees—many, assembled, a wood

therefore. Through the wood
the worn
path, emblematic of Much

Trespass: *Halt. Who goes there?*
A kind of meadow, where it ends
begin trees, from whose twinning

of late light and the already underway
darkness you were expecting perhaps
the stag to step forward, to make

of its twelve-pointed antlers
the branching foreground to a backdrop
all branches;

or you wanted the usual
bird to break cover at that angle
at which wings catch entirely

what light's left,
so that for once the bird isn't miracle
at all, but the simplicity of patience

and a good hand assembling: first
the thin bones, now in careful
rows the feathers, like fretwork,

now the brush, for the laying-on
of sheen . . . *As is always the way,*
you tell yourself, *in*

poems—Yes, always,
until you have gone there,
and gone there, "into the

field," vowing *Only until
there's nothing more
I want*—thinking it, wrongly,

a thing attainable, any real end
to wanting, and that it is close, and that
it is likely, how will you not

this time catch hold of it: flashing,
flesh at once

lit and lightless, a way
out, the one dappled way, back—

Parable

There was a saint once,
he had but to ring across
water a small bell, all

manner of fish
rose, as answer, he was
that holy, persuasive,

both, or the fish
perhaps merely
hungry, their bodies

a-shimmer with
that hope especially that
hunger brings, whatever

the reason, the fish
coming unassigned, in
schools coming

into the saint's hand and,
instead of getting,
becoming food.

I have thought, since, of
your body—as I first came
to know it, how it still

can be, with mine,
sometimes. I think on
that immediate and last gesture

of the fish leaving water
for flesh, for guarantee
they will die, and I cannot

rest on what to call it.
Not generosity, or
a blindness, trust, brute

stupidity. Not the soul
distracted from its natural
prayer, which is attention,

for in the story they are
paying attention. They
lose themselves eyes open.

"All art . . ."

Routinely the sea,
unbuckling, out-
swells the frame it will

return to, be
held restively
by.

If there is a shadow
now, on the water, if
there are several,

somewhere are those that must
cast them, they will not
stay,

what does?
Our bodies, it turns out,
are not flutes, it

is unlikely that
God is a mouth with nothing
better to do than

push a wind
out, across us,
but we are human,

flawed therefore and,
therefore, shall suit ourselves:
Music

Hard Master
I called out,
Undo me, at last

understanding how
gift, any difficult
knot, is—by

fingers, time, patience—
undone, knowing
too the blade by which

—if it means
the best, the most fruit—oh,
let the limbs be cut back.

Hymn

Less the shadow
than you a stag, sudden, through it.
Less the stag breaking cover than

the antlers, with which
crowned.
Less the antlers as trees leafless,

to either side of the stag's head, than—
between them—the vision that must
mean, surely, rescue.

Less the rescue.
More, always, the ache
toward it.

When I think of death, the gleam of
the world darkening, dark, gathering me
now in, it is lately

as one more of many other nights
figured with the inevitably
black car, again the stranger's

strange room entered not for prayer
but for striking
prayer's attitude, the body

kneeling, bending, until it finds
the muscled patterns that
predictably, given strain and

release, flesh assumes.
When I think of desire,
it is in the same way that I do

God: as parable, any steep
and blue water, things that are always
there, they only wait

to be sounded.
And I a stone that, a little bit, perhaps
should ask pardon.

My fears—when I have fears—
are of how long I shall be, falling,
and in my at last resting how

indistinguishable, inasmuch as they
are countless, sire,
all the unglittering other dropped stones.

The Gods Leaving

That they carry away, with them,
vision—this isn't the worst of
the gods leaving: it's that they take

only half. There comes the hour
when—having lain long and favored
at the dark crossroads of Gift

and Desire; having as pliant
swans bested all arrows, no less
at ease with that wreckage than

with the glamour we have learned
to call pain given up to, until
wanted, a dream—we see it

was only, ever, our own bodies
by hands only our strong own
taken here, and here, down, ours

the mouths stalled at *Oh*, the eyes
clearing, enough to read or imagine
a reading for the shadows cast

to nobody's surprise by trees
theatrically there, shifting: *Don't
do this, don't do this*—always,

someone is too late . . . At
that hour, because the gods aren't
indifferent, we rise into what,

already, is the new life—flat,
general, "never for such as
ourselves"—and it seems, at first,

just the old one: rain, the fact
of rain, so ordinary, stepping
into it, I did not think to cry out.

Against His Quitting the Torn Field

Let him put his mouth in the
dust—there may yet be hope.

LAMENTATIONS

"How, entering,
inside him, it became more
easy to believe I would not
breathe the same, it would not be
my life, breathing, breathed
—out, again, ever."

■

There was a bird, once,
like that. Or—

Or, shorn of bird—call only—
a calling-to that seemed
it would never end, be done
raveling.

It starts that way. Likely

■

it goes, somewhere else:

the mouth that says *You can do anything, here*;

the arm tattooed with—
as obviously as if this were
dream—the one word:
Paradise; all in a row, shut

against a frost that, even here, has
place, nine tulips—
seven; oh

and the peonies, or almost, each one
still a fist, which is to say, fat
with chance, or the hard
waking you will have forgotten bone also

■

can be. Somewhere else:

all house lights down.

Rustle of what no longer is required, being shed.

Sounds connoting struggle,
then—

silence? or
—like silence—resolve?

Lights up, on

the male lead, who has just found the body,
the body is someone's
he loved, he can see
it is dead; all the same
does he rock it, and rock it, poor

■

—bird?

There *was* one.
As there will be: yes, another.

Those birds fly well
which have little flesh,
and many feathers.

Though the flesh is
our enemy, we
are commanded to support it.

Of leaves, recall,
were the first garlands woven for
none other than, triumphant, the flesh.

■

Thus, the shield.

She set the clattering bronze down, before him.

Would-Be Everlasting

There is a sea there. Nobody looks at it, or rarely, and even then only
    as, in bed, one turns
occasionally from reading to see the beloved of course there, and of
    course breathing, his
body asleep rises, falls—what different thing is expected?

There, when a body dies, the bereaved assemble and, filling glasses
    with the local drink—
a syrup whose taste, if desire could be made into liqueur, would be
    desire, as bracing as it,
as undiluted with guarantee—they toast over and across the dead.
    Then they leave:

there are other bodies. Prone on the sand, and except for oil naked,
    each making of brow
and muscle a half-nacreous, half-striated dark vow or request, they
    show what it means,
there, to worship—their glossed mouths, too, kept open so as to let
    whatever comes to fill

fill them. For everything there, empty, must be filled, or let go.
    Even the birds understand
this, by whose filling of all the spaces where leaves are no longer,
    the failing tree remains
useful; the ax, for now, passing—

They've a saying there for the heartsick. They say: *however fair still to
    look at, he bears a*
thorn in his throat. They believe the throat is a sieve woven of wounds
    both incurred and
escaped from. By this logic all speech becomes, unsparingly,
    remembrance: we sing, and

we are betrayed . . . How much
was true? Not native to it, how much has from that country been my own
rough translation?

Retreat

FOR MARK AND RANDY

The sea and then, before it, the salted
meadow of sea-hay, the meadow
graven by narrow channels, the more

easy, once, to gain entry, farmers
sailoring into—to cut again down—
the meadow, to harvest the blue, the

green hay which is blond now, which
will for months stand for *Sleeping, Let
be*, the kind of abandon that is endurable

because its ending, if not yet visible,
is nevertheless sure, as much anyway
as all promises: believe them, or

don't believe them, and—then what?
That's history, about the farmers.
Come spring, then summer, the boats

that come instead will be for finding
pleasure because, simply, it's findable
here, and still free, even if, just now,

who will say so? Nobody's here. In
the narrow channels, no pleasuring
boats, either. A single and wooden

dock, yes, but opening out into a space
in which nothing drifts tethered and
waiting, unless memory—what some

plash of want or of need, idling briefly,
makes appear there—counts, waiting.
From inside the meadow, the fidget of

darkness that was, all along, birds
lifts abruptly, assembles: first a shield
thrown, too soon, too recklessly aloft,

then any door by a storm opened, in a
wind swinging, that someone—whom
nobody sees, whom nobody thinks,

therefore, to thank—passes, and—
not tenderly, just—responsibly, pulls
shut. The body first. Then the soul.

The Truth

And now,
the horse is entering
the sea, and the sea

         holds it.

Where are we?

Behind us,
the beach,
        yes, its

scrim,
      yes, of
           grass, dune, sky—Desire

goes by, and though
it's wind of course making
the grass bend,

        unbend, we say
it's desire again, passing
us by, souveniring us with
gospel the grass, turned
choir, leans into,

        Coming—
Lord, soon.

Because
it still matters, to say something. Like:
the heart isn't

      really breakable,
not in the way you mean, any more
than a life shatters,

        —which is what
dropped shells can do, or a bond sworn to,
remember, once

          couldn't, a wooden boat between
unmanageable wave and rock or,
as hard, the shore.

The wooden boat is
not the heart,
      the wave the flesh,
           the rock the soul—

and if we thought so, we have merely been
that long
mistaken.

     Also,
about the shore: it doesn't
mean all trespass
is forgiven, if nightly
the sand is cleared of

any sign
          we were here.

It doesn't equal that whether
we were here or not
matters,
doesn't—

          Waves, because
so little of the world, even
when we say that it has
shifted, has:

same voices,
ghosts, same
hungers come,
          stop coming—

Soon—

How far the land can be found to
be, and
of a sudden,
          sometimes. Now—
so far from rest,
should rest be needed—

Will it drown?

The horse, I mean.

And I—who do not ride, and
do not swim

And would that I had never climbed
its back

And love you too

The Kill

The last time I gave my body up,

to you, I was minded
briefly what it is made of,
what yours is, that

I'd forgotten, the flesh
which always
I hold in plenty no

little sorrow for because—oh, do
but think on its predicament,
and weep.

We cleave most entirely
to what most we fear
losing. We fear loss

because we understand
the fact of it, its largeness, its
utter indifference to whether

we do, or don't,
ignore it. By then, you
were upon me, and then

in me, soon the tokens
I almost never can let go of, I'd
again begin to, and would not

miss them: the swan
unfolding
upward less on trust than

because, simply, that's
what it does; and the leaves,
leaving; a single arrow held

back in the merciless
patience which, in taking
aim, is everything; and last,

as from a grove in
flame toward any air
more clear, the stag, but

this time its bent
head a chandelier, rushing
for me, like some

undisavowable
distraction. I looked back,
and instead of you, saw

the soul-at-labor-to-break-its-bonds
that you'd become. I tensed
my bow:

one animal at attack,
the other—the other one
suffering, and love would

out all suffering—

The Tether

Luck

What we shall not perhaps get over, we
do get past, until—innocent,
with art for once

not in mind, *How did I get here*,
we ask one day, our gaze
relinquishing one space for the next

in which, not far from where
in the uncut grass we're sitting
four men arc the unsaid

between them with the thrown
shoes of horses, luck briefly as a thing
of heft made to shape through

air a path invisible, but there . . .
Because we are flesh, because
who doesn't, some way, require touch,

it is the unsubstantial—that which can
neither know touch nor be known
by it—that most bewilders,

even if the four men at
play, if asked, presumably,
would not say so, any more

than would the fifth man, busy
mowing the field's far
edge, behind me,

his slow, relentless pace promising
long hours before the sorrow
of seeing him go and,

later still, the sorrow
going, until eventually the difficulty
only is this: there was some.

Spoils, Dividing

Thank you for asking—
yes,
I have thought on the soul,

I have decided
it should not be faulted for
its indifference: that is as it

must be.
How blame
the lantern whose limits

always are only the light of
itself, casting the light
out?

That the body enjoys
some moment
in that light, I regard

as privilege.
                Say what
you will.

The hawk's shadow
darkening
the zeroed-in-upon prey,

the victim
classically becoming
quite still—

          It is very
like that. Having
understood which, I admit to

—also—the body as mere
story
whose ending,

like the story itself, is
small—how
not to think, for a time, that it

is not finished,
                    though it
is finished—

The ending was always this one.
Prediction,
gift,

science.
What shines now doesn't, won't
in our lifetime

stop shining—
                    no.
I turned away.

The Point of the Lambs

*The good lambs
in the yellow barn—the rest
housed in blue.* By

"the rest," meaning those who
—the guide explained—inevitably
arrive suffering. *For*

some do, he added.
Soft.
Serious. This—like

a new lesson. As to
some among us, it was,
it seemed. The usual

stammer of heart the naïve
tend to, in the face of what finally
is only the world. What

must it be, to pass
thus—clean, stripped—
through a life? What

reluctance the mind
shows on recognizing
that what it approaches

is, at last, the answer
to the very question it knows
now, but

too late,
oh better to never to have never
put forward. What I

mean is we moved
closer,
in,

to the blue barn's
advertisement—
flaw,

weakness. We
looked in.
Three days, four days

old. Few expected to
finish the evening it was beginning to
be already. And the small

crowd of us
shifting forward, and—
in our shifting uniformly—it

being possible to see how between
us and any
field rendered by a sudden wind

single gesture—kowtow,
upheaval—there was
little difference. Some

took photographs; most
did a stranger thing: touched
briefly, without

distinction, whichever
person stood immediately in
front of, next to. Less

for support than
as remedy or proof or
maybe—given the lambs who,

besides dying, were as well
filthy (disease,
waste and, negotiating

the dwindling contract
between the two,
the flies everywhere)—

maybe the touching
concerned curbing the hand's instinct
to follow the eye, to

confirm vision. Who can
say? I was there—yes—but
I myself touched no one.

Roman Glass

Even in the latter, raveling days of the republic, the Romans clung
    archaically, naïvely
to a belief in equal rule: each year, two consuls were still elected to
    govern—each
equally helpless, inconsequential.

If for nothing else, it's for at least his effectiveness and unwavering
    sense of priority
that Julius Caesar deserves our attention. As example: recognizing the
    folly of equal rule,
he quite efficiently—because literally—saw to the removal of his
    colleague and enemy

Pompey's head. Never mind that he is said not to have given such an
    order, that in public
he displayed revulsion upon being presented the head by his victorious
    army; Caesar is
sure to have admired in the soldiers, if not their loyalty—which virtue
    too, like

beauty, he understood as inherently flawed and therefore subject to
    erosion—then their
precision, their thoroughness, their refusal to compromise any more
    than had the blade
in the executioner's hand. Of course,

Caesar eventually was also murdered—but he prefigures and serves
    as immediate catalyst

for empire, a system which, though bloodier, was nevertheless more
    durable, hypnotic,
and worthy of study, hence the abrupt rise in the number of those
    wanting to chronicle

their own times. Granted, the poetry produced in this period
    remains (with a few
assumable exceptions) negligible in quality; but the prose
    flourishes, especially that which
gets written under the most brutal, and often violent laws of
    censorship. It is as

if restraint (often enough, a naggingly realistic fear for one's life) exerted
    upon prose—
and relentlessly—whatever pressure it is that, in effect, can render a
    poetry *from* prose,
in the way, say, sharded glass becomes other and newly valued, given
    a long enough

exposure to the ocean's necessarily indifferent handling. That piece in
    your hands now
—I found it just south of Rome, not far from the waters that, despite
    pollution, when
they receive the light reflected off the salmon-, sky-, oxblood-
    colored villas that front

the boat-littered bay of Naples, suggest something, still, of a grand
    history that is
finally holy, there being always a holiness attached to that which is
    absolute—even
should the subject prove, the entire time, to have been loss.

Stagger

As when the flesh is shown
to be remarkable
most, for once, because

markless:
where the bruise
was, that we called

a bell, maybe, or
—tipped,
stemless—

a wineglass, or just
the wine spilling
out,

or a lesser lake viewed
from a great height
of air,

instead the surprise that
is blunder when it
has lifted, leaving

the skin to resemble
something like clear
tundra neither foot nor

wing finds,
—or shadow of.
When did the yard get

this swollen—
mint, apples,
like proof of all that

anyway went
on, in our distraction?
When did the room

itself start
stirring with—distant, but
decidedly—the scent of

pines wintering, further
still, a not-very-far
sea—

Regalia Figure

We were mistaken, I think.

I think the soul wants
no mate
except body, what it has

already, I think
the body is not
a cage,

no,

but the necessary foil
against which the soul
proves it was always

true, what they said: to stand
unsuffering
in the presence of another's
agony is its own
perhaps difficult but
irrefutable pleasure.

That I might not have
thought so, without
you, I understand now.

Likewise, about the body
wanting most
only another body, the flesh
from within
lit as if with an instinct for,

endlessly, more
of itself, for
a joint suffering which,

if it too is a kind of pleasure,

if also the only one the body is
likely in this lifetime to

come into, how refuse?

Possibly—probably—there
was not ever a choice
anyway.

The revised version of
effortless.

The twice-plowed-
back-into-itself
field, the light
upon it,

the animal lives
inside the field, inside the light—

I am learning to pity
less what
lacks will entirely.

There are things worse than being
like that. —And yet,
to let go of it, ambition,
seems as impossible, as
impossible—

How extend forgiveness
insincerely? Meeting you,

I knew you utterly.
I saw, utterly,

this life.
I'd put it on.
I'd wear it like

—a crown, for
how it flashes.

Lustrum

Not less; only—different. Not
everything should be visible.
Wingdom:

doves. Not everything
can be. There are many parts
to the body. *The light, like*

I said. Gratia exempli, per
person more than one
heart. As, of hearts,

more than one kind.
As coin.
As thrust. To begin

counting is to understand
what it can mean, to
lose track. Is there nothing

not useful? Anything
left, anymore, private? *Ambition,*
like they said: little torch;

having meant to. Doom is
always in style somewhere
and, where it isn't, will

come back. *Bird*
in the bush, take me. Splendor:
nothing priceless. To believe

anything, to want anything—these,
too, have cost you. *Flame,*
and the beveled sword, set

inside it. This one,
this—what did you think
body was? What did you

mean when you said
not everything should
be said? *The light as a tipped*

cone, searching. The body
that breaks
finally, routinely faltering

before that. *If a sword,*
then without patience; if as
water—pearled, swift. What else

could you have thought,
when you thought
love—having known

the torch, having more than
meant to. *Just watch me.* Not
grand; only—distant. *Weather,*

and the bleachable skull,
set inside it. Locust-wind, small
through-the-yellow-sycamore

fingering wind,
Carry me,
let the prayer—valiant, up—

go. Some bright and
last thing
should.

Tether

I.

Small release—

Bird, risen, flown—

I woke,
all but weightless.

Himself, the weight—exactly—of eclipse.

II.

If the tree looked like insisting upon falling,

    I'd let it fall.

Should you use force, and the forcing
give your skin a red cast as of light to
a night sky,
by which to know there
lies, somewhere,
a towndom,

I'd find the town; enter.

A piece of the wall,
a tower,
refused for a time
fire, and then burned?

    Raise a glass. Grave a stone to it.

III.

Darkest room—

from lightlessness
how slow, homing back—

what required?

    when expect to?

As across a distance, like the one between
this space

and that of God,
no measuring

touches,

quite,

except it fail—

∎

Now he is standing over me

And now I have laid my body on his own

Caravan

Clarion,
boom-time,
yes—though, more often,

the almost-silence that the hum
of activity everywhere
now equals,

cliché, everywhere,
exaggeration,
lines like

It is as if I had known you
forever,
I had only to find you,

images like
water
and sand

and white birds
and—off of all of them—
the light shivering with

meaning, but one that
is difficult to
translate because

language should be—and
is—flexible,
it recalls, in

this way, morality,
how there's nothing, it
seems, not to be given

in to. Some
are swimming,
others scavenging

—coins,
            shells—
others struggle across

blankets whose
stones-as-anchors
routinely fail

at a new corner.
The corners at first
fluttering like truth, then

like the edges we
imagine for it.
I have been here before,

apparently. I am leading the way.

The Figure, the Boundary, the Light

As he crosses the field, he is
easily all I mean by *the flesh
is small, is occasional*:

the grass he divides with
his body reuniting behind him
like too immediate a forgiveness;

even those birds that are least
remarkable do not notice, and
transcend him.

              Questions like
*What is the difference between
intention and that space to which*

*any bird—merely and next—
comes?*
          To ask which, means

finally to resolve little, and lose
time. He has reached, almost,
the field's ending, which is trees:

birch, aspen; a third I cannot
call dissuasion, for he is entering,
has gone in.

　　　　　　　Undeliberately,
on purpose.
　　　　　As I have seen

before, a man touching what
he has not lost, but expects to.
The parts that are visible as,

already, the parts that are more
few. Like proof, omen, both,
just his hair, now—despite

shadow, still a brightness; its
dimming, that of anything—
chance,

　　　　　when it moves away.
As I understand it, I could
call him. Though it would help,

it is not required that I give him
a name first. Also, nothing
says he stops, then, or must turn.

Revision

Which is worse—not being
myself, for long hours, able to

account for my own absence; or
not having been, by anyone,

asked to—I can't say. As when
the leaves have but to angle

in direct proportion to the wind's
force, times its direction,

and the mind, whose
instinct is to resist any

namelessness, calls
all of it—leaves, leaves,

and the wind's force—
trust, at first, then *disregard*

until, suspecting the truer name is
neither of these, it must

stop naming. Or as in
the days, reportedly, of

the gods having dwelled
among us—always

people invariably not knowing
and then (some irreducible

odor, an abrupt
solidity to the light) only then

knowing, but too late,
their faces changed

forever after by the difficult
weight of mere witness,

of having none but their own
word for it . . . If mistake, possibly,

yet mistake this
afternoon seems less

a river than a barely contained in
spite of everything

belief: there's another ending.
In this one, I recognize you—

and the recognizing has the effect of
slowing down that

part of me that would
walk past, or as if away toward

another ending—   You

speak first. And I'll answer.

Rock Harbor

Golden

There, behind the raised
and extended
wing to which
no bird
no fiend
no haloing is
attached: two bodies,

fucking. It is difficult
to see, but that much—
from the way, with great
then greater
effort, their mouths
seem half to recall or
want to

a song even older,
holier than the one they
fill with—I can
guess. The rest,
I know: that it's dream;
that, in dream,
to know a thing is to

have a gift and
not to, especially. Like
refusing to prove what

anyway all scrutable
signs point to. Stopped
trees are the least of it,
the still standing

but decidedly aslant
version of unanimous,
what looks at
first like approbation;
then—like trees,
and how a wind will
pass through. To turn

with and not
against it
no more means
the wind is with us than
the gods are. I don't
believe each gets what
each deserves.

As a Blow, from the West

Names for the moon:
Harvest; and Blue; and
Don't Touch Me—

and Do. I dreamed I had
made a home on the side
of a vast, live volcano,

that the rest was water,
that I was one among many of
no distinction: we but

lived there, like so many
birds that, given the chance
not to fly for once in

formation, won't take it, or
cannot, or—or—but
what of choice can a bird know?

Down the volcano's sides,
in the pose of avalanche
except frozen, and so

densely it seemed impossible
they should not strangle
one another—yet they

did not—grew all
the flowers whose names
I'd meant to master;

it was swift, the dream—so
much, still, to catch
up to—though I could not

have known that, of course,
then: isn't it only in
the bracing and first wake of

loss that we guess most cleanly
the speed with which what held us
left us? In the dream, the world

was birdless, lit, yielding, it
seemed safe, which is not to say
you weren't in it. You were, but

changed somewhat, not so much
a man of few words,
more the look of one who

—having entered willfully
some danger, having just returned
from it—chooses instead

of words his body as
the canvas across which to
wordlessly broadcast his coming

through. We lived
in a manner that—if it
didn't suggest an obliviousness

to a very real and always-there
danger—I would call heady;
it was not that. Think,

rather, of the gods: how,
if they do in fact know
everything, they must understand

also they will be eventually
overthrown by a new order,
which is at worst a loss

of power, but not of life,
as the gods know it. I was
not, that is, without

ambition: the illicit, in
particular, I would make it
my business to have studied;

and of that which is gained
easily, to want none
of it. Flowers; names

for the moon. It was
swift, the dream, the body
a wordless and stalled

avalanche that, since forgivable—
if I could—I would forgive, poor
live but flagging, dying now

volcano. And the water
around its sides receding with
a dream's swiftness: everywhere,

soon, sand and sand, a desert that,
because there was no water,
and because they missed it,

the natives had called a sea, and
to the sea had given a name:
Friendship, whose literal

translation in the country of
dream is roughly "that which
all love evolves

down to"—

Until to leave, or
try to—and have drowned

trying—becomes refrain,
the one answer each time
to whatever question:

what was the place called?

what was the house like?

what was it we did inside it?

how is it possible that it cannot be enough to have given
up to you now the dream as—for a time, remember—I did give

my truest self? why won't you take it—if a gift, if yours?

The Clearing

Had the light
changed, possibly—or,

differently, was that how I'd
seen it

      always, and not
looking? Was I meant for

a vessel? Did I only
believe so and,

so, for a time, was it true but

only in that space which belief makes
for its own wanting?

What am I going to
do with you
         —Who just

said that?

Whose the body—where—that voice
belongs to?

Might I turn,
toward it, whinny

into it?

My life
a water,

or a cure for
that which no water
can cure?

His chest
a forest, or a lush
failure—

Even now, shall I choose? Do I
get to?

Dearest-once-to-me

Dearest-still-to-me

Have I chosen
already,

or is choice a thing
hovering yet, an

intention therefore, from
which, though
late, could I hurry back?

*What am I going to do with you—*or

how?
Whom for?

         If stay my hand—where

rest it?

By Hard Stages

All the glories—
ribbed, and
separate,

       collective
sway-in-the-wind.
Shut them.

       To have wanted
more, where has that
carried me,

       if what
so much matters
now can be proven

later to all
along have been doomed
not to?

       ■

       The governing
drift was from
sensation to

       distraction to
irrelevance: "they came
to nothing," it says here,

"en route
settling for things like
heat falling mostly

against, light mainly
falling, between them
a bush or

a skull
shimmering like another
example of absence of

will—with
heat only,
shivering—"

■

Do I make
a difference? or
What is it

so persuades, I
must make one?
The text breaks like a road

forking where none
warned of . . .
Look at yourself,

Look at you.
Have I not
looked there—

possibility for
—into it?
How small,

■

without effort almost,
can be the leap from
it-is-findable to

we-have-found-it.
Though not water,
not the flash, even,

as if off of that which
could be water, could
also not be—

To have
called it water. "They
crossed themselves,

they gave
utterly themselves over
to what

wasn't there,
that it might
save, or drown them . . ."

The Clarity

No dream—but as

if so, moving at first
with the force of

idea purely; and
then of a man convinced
he has justified

brilliantly himself to
himself; and then
of the yearling that,

haltered at
last, remains
still to be gentled, to be

broken-to-ride, although
no yearling, not a horse
ever, and not dream.

I turned.
I could see,
across the room,

heaped there like fouled
linen like memory like
detritus stepped

away from, the truth of
—of myself: glintless,
yes, but no

more so for my having (how
long?) disavowed it.
Suggestive of sorrow,

or the cool irreversibility that
attaches commonly to
larger mistakes

of judgment—so did it
lie there: undiminished.

I take it, in the darkness, to my face.

To Break, to Ride

That, nightly,
some blooms fold,
some open; how

the opossum at the same
hour forages the same swatch
of yard; and the moth,

a shadow, all
over again navigates
more shadow—

There's a knowing born
of conquering;
conscious at first,

or never, reflexive finally,
a mastery of pattern,
how a thing changes—

light,
a difference in it,
an absence of—

the better to mark and
react in turn to
when, of a sudden, pattern

stops: where
is danger?
what is safe? This

kind of knowing, it is like
a ladder. It is
scales, in music:

though I believe that the earth
rotates, what I
notice more is

the moon appearing,
what I'd rather
remember is another

story—concerns a boat,
routine, the bearing
away of one

brightness, the fact
of others,
smaller, more of. How

still, beside me. The difference
between us the same as
that between a garden

shaped by patience,
attention,
plan,

and a field to which
an unexpected heat in late
October brings

now the worker bees
confused, instinctive,
back. If a sadness

to it, then
a sadness, one that
no more lets me go than

I let *it* go. It is waste,
to worry. We shall never
be more close than we are now.

Trade

Bending—as no
flower bends—
casting the difficult rule

of his attention upon an elsewhere
that accordingly broke open
into a splendor that, too,

would pass,
I am resigned,
mostly,

said the emperor,
to a history between us less of loss than,
more protractedly, of losing—

and, having said as much, said
nothing else to the man to
whom he'd said it;

whom, for years now, he'd called
variously paramour,
consort,

sir; who, for
himself, said nothing;
who from where he was seated could

see, and easily,
each at its labeled and color-coded slip
moored slackly,

the bows of the ships of the Fleet
Imperial, about which
what he found, just

then, most worth admiring it
is impossible, anymore, to
say exactly:

the trim of them,
flawless, sleek—reminiscent, in
that way, of almost any line from Ovid; or

when there was wind,
how the bows tipped,
idly,

in it;
or the stillness, afterwards,
that they found; or the way they seemed to.

Return to the Land
of the Golden Apples

Blue wash. The winged horses look
like horses—artless, free
of connotation. They hide

just now their wings,
or they forget, or do not
think to make

much more of a gift
for flight than
of the water viewable

behind them—a sea,
a lake—
which they ignore, pulling

at the record-of-where-a-wind-was,
the now-resist-now-don't,
and other flowers

whose growth has even
outstripped the grass, the colors
wind as far as the ruined tower, up

even to the room that
crowns it, over the half moss, half
ledge of window, glassless,

into the room, which is small,
not empty: the body,
and a mirror. Inside

the mirror, the body
turning, stopping
—sometimes the way, in

sudden shadow, will any
animal; sometimes,
as the hero stops

in the gathering light of reputation
he soon must recognize
is his own. The body

inside the mirror, turning,
singing *I am the one who forces,
I am the one who stays*

*to watch,
I am the grit gone somehow
shine, the blow,*

the forced thing, opening
—Singing inside the mirror,
to no one, to

itself, the body folding, and
unfolding—as if
map, then shroud—its song.

Fretwork

Reports are various—
conflicting also:

many fell,
    a few;

like taken cities . . .

    ■

Whether or not
to any loss there is weight
assignable,

    or a music given

—some play of notes,
slow-trumpeted,

for which to listen
is already to be
too late;

    whether forgetting is
or is not proof of
mercy, henceforth let

others say.

■

       Is not victory itself
the proof of victory?

■

Little hammer, chasing—onto
unmarked metal—pattern,
decoration,

a name,

a scar upon the face
of history, what

has no face

■

       Of briar
and thorn, my bed.

■

—I stand in clover.

Halo

In the dream, as if to remind
himself of his own power—that he
does have some—the gelding

whinnies once,
once more, at
nothing passing.

If this were song, I'd call it *Someone*
Waving from Across the Water
at Someone Else

Not Waving Back,
but it is dream. You, speaking; and I
distracted as usual

from the words, this time by
how you speak them;
the way tuberoses open,

or new leafage—
slow, instinctive; sexual
vaguely.

There is little I've not done for you.
There are questions.
There are answers I do not give.

Between the sometimes terrible
(because leaving us always) fact
of the body to which we're

each, each moment, eroded
down—between our bodies
and the pattern the light,

dreamlight, is making on them,
the effect is one of trade routes
long since confused by time, war,

a forgetfulness, or
because here, and here, as from
much handling, the map

especially has gone soft:
wind as a face gone red with blowing,
oceans whose end is broken stitchery—

swim of sea-dragon, dolphin,
shimmer-and-coil, invitation . . . You know
the kind of map I mean. Countries as

distant as they are believable,
than which—to find,
to cross—I am not

more difficult. *Here I am*, I say,
wanting to help,
Over here. And you turn. And

on its axis—swift,
inexorable as luck—the dream turning,
with you . . .

The Rest of Love

Custom

There is a difference it used to make,
seeing three swans in this versus four in that
quadrant of sky. I am not imagining. It was very large, as its
effects were. Declarations of war, the timing fixed upon for a
    sea-departure; or,
about love, a sudden decision not to, to pretend instead to a kind
of choice. It was dramatic, as it should be. Without drama,
what is ritual? I look for omens everywhere, because they are
    everywhere
to be found. They come to me like strays, like the damaged,
something that could know better, and should, therefore—but
    does not:
a form of faith, you've said. I call it sacrifice—an instinct for
    it, or a habit at first, that
becomes required, the way art can become, eventually, all we
    have
of what was true. You shouldn't look at me like that. Like one
    of those saints
on whom the birds once settled freely.

Singing

Overheard,
late, this morning: *Don't blame*
me, if I am everything your heart
has led to.

Hazel trees;
ghost-moths in the hazel branches.
Why not stay?

It's a dream I've had
twice now: God is real, as
the difference between
having squandered faith and having lost it
is real. He's straightforward:

when he says *Look at me when I'm speaking*,
it means he's speaking.
He's not unreasonable:

because I've asked, he shows me his mercy—
a complicated arrangement
of holes and

hooks, buckles. *What else did you think*
mercy looked like,

he says and, demonstrating, he straps it on, then takes it off.

Vow

Unpatterned rustling,
the kinds of trees—pine,
scrub oak—you'll have
seen before.

Is it latchless, or only
unlatched,
that door,
slamming?

By *disarray*,
I mean the look findable
in the eyes of a horse in storm,
and panicking.

What I mean by *luster*:
look,
see the black of its mane?

Thunder,
a lasso coming close, that
just misses.

Manured hay bales;
dirt the damp has kept,
days now,
from traveling far.

As far as conquest?
No. Not that far.

As far as the urge to
rise and begin conquering? No,

farther.
Incongruities.
Tiger lilies—
little slaves, little

slaves in the light—
as an example. Words
to a childhood song
I'd thought forgotten, but

parts come back. I lie down.
I wear nothing at all.

Like Stitches Where the Moths
Have Made an Opening

Star-in-the-hand   Cupped fire   Fist,
luminous.
            What keeps staying lost is not,
anymore, the thing itself, but the definition
it once provided,
                  as history does to what
occurs—to what has not, yet.
                        Leafe-gold, what is
blown—is blowable—*away.*
                        God enters me
as if from behind; he shakes, inside me. *I want*
what you want, he says. I say *Why regard what I*
can't choose? To be anchorless,
                              but not unanchored:
To have failed means, at worst, once we flourished,
that's right, isn't it?
                  Windfall whose imperfections
fade in a shabby harvest, the body—as again from
mistakes all the same enjoyed—lifts, staggers,
like light
            off spokes of a wheel set spinning,
                                    as the wheel
slows down: speed of legend, of the myth that follows,
of the life that a myth eclipses. Speed of
                              Don't.
Not now. Listen: someone is calling my name.

Late Apollo

I.

Brief in the light of streetlamp, then back again,
into dark—two boys, throwing a ball between them.
The younger one is almost handsome, a star
already, going down.
                    At last the snow lies
unoracular,

unstepped across.
               If I could speak, I'd speak
to no one, now. I'd remember the way everyone
else does: later, when none of it matters,
memory as good as a mirror for changing things,
no good at all:

          You're in a garden,
you've trellised the dwarf cherry, trained it so as,
branching, to become—and cast in shadow against the wall—
this fan, opening, held open, the way a map is held
in wind—

          The map makes the getting there
at first look easy: a prairie, then the mountains, then the sea.

II.

And now it is as we wanted it.
And now they are very still:

the grapes, rampant once;
                              the roses that—
like grace—require no training
to swag and scramble;
                              the waters there . . .

A stillness like that of music resting—or sex,
after: what they call sadness, though it
is not sadness.

                    Country to which, increasingly, I've
felt native. I believe
I could—

                    Like asking at first *Where am I*
after dream—and the room, in pieces, slow,
comes back:
                    a language that, all this time, we knew.

Here comes the word for mystery.
Here is the word for true.

III.

As if everything were in the effect, finally.
Less the wind itself, than a quickness,
or lack of it, with which the gulls, lifting,

move forward; or how the trees, here at
shoreline, recall or don't the startled angle
of retreat-before-temptation that is fixed,

apparently, instinctive in the saint—this is
how, in the old, illuminated paintings,
the saints most easily can be picked out

from the crowd around them, the crowd
whose purpose, I think, must be to remind us
that the world is larger, will always be larger

than its exceptions. The crowd equals
what's forgettable. The light, for as far as
I can see, is that of any number of late

afternoons I remember still: how the light
seemed a bell; how it seemed I'd been living
inside it, waiting— I'd heard all about

that one clear note it gives.

All It Takes

Any force—
generosity, sudden updraft.
Fear. Things invisible,

and the visible effects by which
we know them. Human gesture. Betrayed,
betrayed. The dampness of fog as

understandable by how, inside it, from within their
thicket of nowhere left to hide—
that leafless—the winter berries, more than usual,

shine. First always
comes the ability to believe, and then the need to.
The ancient Greeks; the Romans after. How they

made of love a wild god; of fidelity—a small,
a tame one. I am no less grateful for
the berries than for the thorns that are

meant, I think, to help. As if
sometimes the world really did amount to
a quiet arrangement. Cut flowers. Make

death the one whose eyes are lidless. And
—already—you are leaving. You have
crossed the water.

White Dog

First snow—I release her into it—
I know, released, she won't come back.
This is different from letting what,

already, we count as lost go. It is nothing
like that. Also, it is not like wanting to learn what
losing a thing we love feels like. Oh yes:

I love her.
Released, she seems for a moment as if
some part of me that, almost,

I wouldn't mind
understanding better, is that
not love? She seems a part of me,

and then she seems entirely like what she is:
a white dog,
less white suddenly, against the snow,

who won't come back. I know that; and, knowing it,
I release her. It's as if I release her
because I know.

Fervor

Somewhere between
To Be Lit
and To Be

Transfigured,
he'd removed his shirt,
his shoes,

he had opened his pants;
he wore nothing under.

I did what I do—

pretended to be a fallen gate,
its hinges gone, that
soon the snow,

continuing, must hide
most of.

Is this how it will finish?
Is fervor belief's
only measure? Is there

no saving
what betrays itself?

After which,
I held him
until his body was not

his body,
was a single birch
I'd seen years ago—

down, and silvering,
in a field,

Indiana.

Sleep, I said. But he
couldn't sleep;
he said *Tell me a story.*

*There was once
a mockingbird*, I told him, *It
knew no better:*

it would sing.

It sang all night . . .

Fresco: Cove and Spur

The stone rises, with its runes, from the sea.

If I remember it, did it happen?

Part horse,
part man, dragging
away by the hair
the bride who, alone in the scene, lifts
no cry.

      Here, as token of thanks for
how the withered limb was made
strong again,

how the infant swam miraculously
free of the raft
of blindness,

each has left his particular
mark, that the stone
carries easily,
each as weightless
as a scar
is weightless,

if nobody stares, is it
gone?
Is it?

Graffito—

Tattoo,

      what changes as the flesh it
adorns changes, until
the image itself
has grown distorted past
all recognition save
that of memory: here, once,

was the reveler—
cap-and-bells,

beads; here, the stitcher of leather
into release, restraint,
costume; and here,

part horse, part man,
fallen already, having
shoved already his way
up, from behind
into and—

and into—.

Familiar light

The stone

The sea

As when all photographs
prove nothing.

I have known a man
to rouse from within
the wind-rifled field of
long fever,

he'll rise,

he'll take eagerly
the cool water, he appears,
at first, most restored . . .

If a Wilderness

Then spring came:
                    branches-in-a-wind . . .

I bought a harness, I bought a bridle.
I wagered on God in a kind stranger—
kind at first; strange, then less so—
and I was right.
                    The difference between
God and luck is that luck, when it leaves,
does not go far: the idea is to believe
you could almost touch it . . .

                              Now he's
singing, cadence of a rough sea— A way of
crossing a dark so unspecific, it seems
everywhere: isn't that what singing, once,
was for?
          I lay the harness across my lap,
the bridle beside me for the sweat—the color
and smell of it—that I couldn't, by now,
lift the leather free of, even if I wanted to.

I don't want to.

Here, on Earth

When the battle, like favor, shifts
in Greek epic, there are smaller signs inside
the large ones:
          an otherwise random soldier,
around whom none of the story apparently
figures, has removed

          his headgear, its horsehair plume
stirs barely, and it is fate
and a breeze only, *Never again* and *Sure,*
          why not—

both, and neither.
          Everything,
as always in epic, has changed forever.

Moth, consuming what is dearest to it— There
is a glamour,
          even to a thing undoing itself,
there is— Sing it:

One of them was sucking the others—in turn, slowish—off.

A kiss where roughly, in the dark, his brow should be.

II.

If out of the distance between descent

                     and the memory of it

could be spun a thread,

I'd make a softness,

             I'd be the tortoiseshell boat

wrapped soft

        inside it, where nothing shines.

That was yesterday. There's little

that won't sound reasonable

             for a time. Then reason passes,

the speed of traveling

          stays constant,

we have merely become, ourselves,

               more conscious of it.

Only days ago, the peonies opened—and already—

Just look at them: group portrait

of a winter river the thaw

           has touched,

and now takes hold of—and soon must possess entirely.

III.

As if I were afraid, as if I should be, as after
a series of blows
                    staggered back from in a wind

all crash and spray, like struck
water, and the wind had spoken:
"The body as hieroglyph for silence"—what does

that mean? and
                    What if discretion is
not a blade—dropped, retrieved—that we drop again?

Radiance unrelenting—
no peace, no shadow,
no shelter now—

                    I clap my hands
over all of it: *what's ruined?*
                              what isn't yet?

I clap my hands: a field, and as if I'd fallen here before,
and I'd forgotten.
                    That's not possible—

You carried me. You took me. You hid your face.

Like Cuttings for a Wreath
of Praise and Ransom

Abbreviation,
            part that gives what is left
away. As if released,
                  a stone—as from
a sling. The landscape opening as if no end to it,
a longing anywhere
                  for some resistance, some
stop: the magnolia, its ring of bird-ravaged
seed-cones,
            the birds themselves, a wind lifting
a collar of feathers at the neck of each—stiff
courtiers,
            Elizabethan. Clarity, versus
blur.
      Fine distinctions.
                        Not, it seems,
the cries of joy. Not punishment—think
in terms of, instead,
                  persuasion. Silo, through which
the rains, passing,
                  pass unimpeded. Hunger,
versus the pursuit of it. That's what they say.
With time, with wear,
                  the leather softening. They say
the legs go here. The straps adjust.
                              Like so.

Fray

There it lay, before me, as they had
said it would: a distance
I'd wish to cross,

then try to, then leave
off wishing. Words like *arc*,
and *trajectory*. And *push*. The words

themselves over time
coming to matter
the way, in painting, color does: less,

finally, than the gesture
each stroke
memorializes.

A kind of sleep
that will look like death,
they said,

A kind of waking that will look
bewildered.
I woke,

as it were. I was not
bewildered. The distance as uncrossed
as it had been,

but now a clarity—like that
of vision. A kind of crossing.
Parts that the light

reached, relative
to everything else, what the light
kept missing. Spirea

in a wind; wind in the spirea's
leggy branches—I could make
distinctions: weeping

spruce; weeping maple. I could love you
as I had loved you—as only
humans can love each other: it's

a human need,
to give to shapelessness
a form.

Riding Westward

(2006)

Bright World

—And it came to pass, that meaning faltered; came detached
unexpectedly from the place I'd made for it, years ago,
fixing it there, thinking it safe to turn away, therefore,
to forget—hadn't that made sense? And now everything
did, but differently: the wanting literally for nothing
for no good reason; the inability to feel remorse at having
cast (now over some, now others), aegis-like, though it
rescued no one, the body I'd all but grown used to waking
inside of and recognizing, instantly, correctly, as mine,
my body, given forth, withheld, shameless, merciless—
for crying shame. Like miniature versions of a lesser
gospel deemed, over time, apocryphal, or redundant—both,
maybe—until at last let go, the magnolia flowers went on
spilling themselves, each breaking open around, and then
apart from, its stem along a branch of stems and, not of
course in response, but as if so, the starlings lifting, unlifting,
the black flash of them in the light reminding me of what I'd
been told about the glamour of evil, in the light they were
like that, in the shadow they became the other part, about
resisting evil, as if resistance itself all this time had been
but shadow, could be found that easily . . . *What will you do?*
Is this how you're going to live now? sang the voice in my
head: singing, then silent—not as in desertion, but as
when the victim suddenly knows his torturer's face from
before, somewhere, and in the knowing is for a moment
distracted, has stopped struggling— And the heart gives in.

Radiance versus Ordinary Light

Meanwhile the sea moves uneasily, like a man who
suspects what the room reels with as he rises into it
is violation—his own: he touches the bruises at each
shoulder and, on his chest,
                          the larger bruise, star-shaped,
a flawed star, or hand, though he remembers no hands,
has tried—can't remember . . .
                          That kind of rhythm to it,
even to the roughest surf there's a rhythm findable,
which is why we keep coming here, to find it, or that's
what we say. We dive in and, as usual,
                          the swimming
feels like that swimming the mind does in the wake
of transgression, how the instinct to panic at first
slackens that much more quickly, if you don't
look back. Regret,
                          like pity, changes nothing really, we
say to ourselves and, less often, to each other, each time
swimming a bit farther,
                          leaving the shore the way
the water—in its own watered, of course, version
of semaphore—keeps leaving the subject out, flashing
Why should it matter now and *Why,*
                          why shouldn't it,
as the waves beat harder, hard against us, until that's
how we like it, I'll break your heart, break mine.

Ocean

Is the voyage over? This, the lull I've come to expect
after smaller victories, stunning blows of defeat? Or is this
but respite? The water has stopped its shifting, the ship
follows suit— Aboard the ship, like a hand abandoning
one gesture for another as the mind directs it, so
as the captain commands them the sailors variously
settle or, lifting themselves free from their having settled,
they rise to an attention that proves obedience can be a form
of love. He passes among them like a brightness, like
what he is: a man for whom they'd do anything, they're
a theft in readiness, magnolia forced too soon open—
split signatures, so many bruises on a freakish branch,
nodding, windless—they obey him as if divinity were
but one of several irreversible truths about him that each

had swallowed. They believe what he believes, without
exception: *There's a courtesy to be found everywhere—*
worth finding, the slightest act, his removing the cross from
around his neck before fucking a stranger, a grace almost—
why not believe that, having watched him, having been
instructed to? *There's a life after death. Each comes*
back to the world transformed, not human—some lesser
animal. The captain has told them already he'll return
as a horse—and swiftly, steadily, they do imagine it:
the captain rearing, his raised hooves casting about at the air
before finding the earth again, crushing the grass each
sailor hopes desperately he'll come back as—has every
intention to—a field and powerless, the captain a horse
the field contains now, now doesn't, may never again . . .

Brocade

As when the vine, climbing,
twisting—
as if would strangle—

doesn't, instead
ends each time in proof
of how to end is—or can be—

to be transformed: blue flower,
and then a bugle; then a mouth gone
blue with having meant to swallow,

not spill, not like this, the names
escaping, the ground
shelving, almost as if with the kind

of tenderness that hovers
over scant acquaintance
as it comes undone, silently,

mutually, regret
nowhere figuring, or not any
longer as an emotion, more

the inverse of one, as gesture
is memory's inverse,
memory given the properties

briefly of a body when it passes upward
and as if unstoppably through a heaven
of air, now you steady me,

and now you don't, surface
as of a pond I've crossed
often, have laid my head against,

body of winter in whom
the limbs of the trees crack
like favor, cold

into which I speak because
I *can* speak, making distinctions
because between to know

and to understand
there is still a difference,
suffering-as-pleasure

is not the suffering that must
make keen again what
pleasure has blunted, which I

believe, we shall want
for nothing, I believe that too,
or almost, why shouldn't I say so,

some admit to flaw, some sway
inside it, sing softly,
the better to bring a far thing

near, they tell me,
I tell myself, I sing as I can,
softly, as I sway among them.

Island

Sea lavender, in staggered flower—
As for the sea: like a truce meant to last
only until each party has fittingly dismissed its dead—that's
how still it was. And the mind, without
having at all wondered if it could,

                              or how, moved elsewhere,
to where nothing as I'd understood it, as I'd been
given to understand it, could help, because none of it—
the handling of light as a form of prosody, the body
as body, the soul as a lantern swung, swingable against
competing darknesses, *Who goes there?* and *Who
has not?*—none of it was true. There was no worse
or better part of me—

                    Like choosing which one to be forever
changed into: the invisible sycamore, in fullest leaf,
or the equally invisible horse tied slackly to it.
Not wish; being forced to choose—and the only mercy,
that the end will be swift, irrevocable, and at first look easy. I looked
at you.

Bow Down

I.

As if he, too, could see the world,
just in front of us,
coming divided: those who step
routinely toward a dark that, mostly,
has seemed avoidable;

those who let them—

               World from which,

if for no other reason, then
out of pity, I should
look away.

Out of decency.

I should try, or should seem to have tried, or to be about to.

II.

If I don't go to him, if I do nothing, if he comes to me first,
and then I follow: does it count as trespass? Should it?
If he bends aside the lower branches— If I pass unmarked

beneath them— If I look away, as if toward something
difficult, bright, and departing always, like the parts of
memory that, very briefly, flare as what is remembered grows

more far; if I look away, and he does—if I could do that—
where does the damage go to, if damage figures here, if
no one sees it—no, if no one looks at it, if my stroking his

hair back also figures, gently, if I shall miss him, if I do already,
broad strokes, consolation, though there is nothing to console
him for, nothing, why cry out, if the mud washes easily, if

the bruise eventually undoes itself, if somewhere a kindness
still counts as anything, let it count as kindness, why ruin it
by saying otherwise, why even speak of it, why speak at all?

Once, to ask
meant a small departure, and then
a larger one, shape of going—far,
away. As where the meadow led.
Red of switchgrass. A calf by the rope
toward slaughter.
Did that happen? Do you
wish it had? Why should the saints stand
apart from me, as if between us, suddenly,
they could see a difference? Questions fell
the way water did, off of—no,
away from your body as, sometimes,
I would still remember it: you
making of your hand now a fist,
now a dove where it finds my chest—has
found it—and after, settling. The descent
was easy. It always is. It always
has been. Think twice, or don't. Given
the face of God in front of them, some
look away, others look once
and know a blindness
ever after. Will it have been worth it?
Was it? Wasn't it? Is it only a wind,
or my own voice, stuttering now
against me? *Bow down, inside*

the shadows here, and know a peace that leaves
elsewhere all human understanding of what,
earlier, peace looked like, it seems
to say. No. I say so. Saying it, as if
into a wind. No. As if into the shadow-work
that is all, I think, the body will have
meant—each time keeps meaning: canopy,
leaves above me, something that
almost I can see around, though
not through, the leaves
muttering, where a wind lets them, where a wind
makes them, *Come here, clipped bird,*
spattered stag whose flank the shaft entered
easily—come here. And forget. And sleep.

After

A bell swings, in darkness.

          Dark, like the bottom of the well
of childhood, up the steep walls of which I'd spend hours shouting
words like *anthracite, ginkgo*—over and over, each word falling
back to me, until it stayed, and was mine: yes, that dark. And yet—
though it's dark, in the darkness through which the bell swings

I can tell it's fall again, the usual fireless fire the leaves make
as they give themselves over, first from their branches, then
a second time when—crushable, as the diminished tend almost as
willingly, it seems, as instantly to become—they give way beneath
and around those of us who have places to go, still, and believe
in getting there.

          A bell swings; then darkness. —Is dying like this?

The bells in my head swing their own heads, their difficult black clappers
for tongues swing against them in turn, like memory, which is a wave
hitting shore.

To a Legend

Stargazer lilies, marguerites. But you
must have dreamt that. The field is
clearer now than you've ever seen it—

founders, as it should. As it must.
And the light passes over it; of course
it does. Makes visible what wasn't:
deer scat; fox run. Pocketknife: not

lost after all. You can leave any time.
Stand up in the field   Lie down in it
Come here   And you do what they

tell you to. Strangers. Your body
includes them, the way light includes
everything it passes over, briefly.
And briefly defines: now you're

the horse, now the snow that veils it,
now the wild signature that the horse
keeps making, startled, inside the snow;

and now its rider—untrained, uncertain,
both. And the horse somewhere
understanding this. Somewhere inside—

as a field continues, far, past the part
that's seen of it. Something at once
still and rampant, as across the field
of a coat-of-arms that any field, seen

from above, makes sometimes. Even
flowerless. Of course it does. Even
foxless, and strange. You can do what

you want, and no hand stopping you,
the field that clear, and you as alone,
inside it, as ever before. You making
your own small, inadvertent shadows

around the light as you fall through it.
As fall you must. Blue wrist over
shin over ankle. On a ground of stars.

The Messenger

What is it you had meant to say? What had
I said?
      And the snow fell to the same as usual
transfigurational effect, making the world seem
not the world, very briefly, and then what it
always is again: just the world—changed,
changeable.
      What happens, I think, is we betray
ourselves first—our better selves, I'd have said once—
and the others after, as if that made knowing
what to call it somehow easier, meaning less
unkind.
      Why give it a name? What makes me
want to?
      There's a bell tower near here
I'd meant to show you, how there's still a music
hearable, despite the bell itself missing—lost,
or stolen, though it is difficult to steal a bell
so large, presumably,
         and a shame to lose one.
I'd meant to show you that.
      Wind enters and leaves
the tower like a thing that lives there—but nobody
lives there, no one, I keep meaning to say.

Forecast

Betrayal, all along, will have been the least of it.
Some fall like empire—slowly, from the wild, more
unmappable borders inward, until reduced to history,
to the nothing from which, in the end,

                              history's made;
and others, they fall with the dizzying swiftness of
one of those seized-in-the-night

                         kingdoms—chambers
awash with the blood of princelings, their spattered
crowns toys now in the conqueror's

                            fine hands . . . As for
the common choice, the rote of exile that most call a life,
days on end spent muttering about loyalty, tattooing
the word *Who?* over one nipple, *Why?* just below the other,
foraging

            shirtless among the animals or, worse, only
watching them pass—blind, but for instinct—beneath
the stooped cathedrals that the trees make in a storm
that—forever, it seems—looks permanent: No. Even
slaughter will have been better, I think,

                       than that.

Translation

Stillness of a body that seizure has just finished visiting, has

passed through. The trees, I mean. Oranges. Figs, and lemons. I forget
the dream that I'd had beneath them, only that I'd had one.
I woke from it. Nothing anywhere lacked definition.
Like vision in pieces, scattered, and now reconnoitering. You asleep
beside me. This life as a mown field contained by wilderness,

the wilderness ringed in turn loosely by possibility
in the form of countless unchecked stands of pliant grasses
in a wind forever ready to stop blowing, though it doesn't, ever, it doesn't
seem to— I watched you sleeping. All was stillness. I watched

your eyes keep not unshutting. The rest would happen
once you'd opened them. Bluish moths, strawberries, blue flowers. The
    rest you know.

Break of Day

Though it came close, conquest never
quite began to describe it, and now
nothing does—to try to would mean having

somewhere to admit to vision being what,
more and more, it seems, a thing to be
panned for from the very wreckage

over which, for a time, vision skimmed, had
darted . . . Not conquest, more like pillaging:
the stripping of bodies, then the storming

of them, face up, face down, preference
mattering then, as now, apparently.
The year in the usual way unravels, leaves

fill the yard, you can see now the thickness
of vine that, all summer long, strangled
the pear tree, still strangles it, has grown

into the trunk in places—doesn't this, too,
count as intimacy, can't it—you can see
the stunted fruit hanging there useless,

unable to fall, so much work to be done,
and done with, why should you be
exceptional? Not conquest, but a kind of

joy at last, wasn't it, even if joy only
in its smaller, more common forms—
It had seemed enough, you say to yourself

as you might to a stranger and, a little sadly,
it seems that it was enough, though what
stirs now, inside you, isn't sadness but

sexual, you recognize it by its bracing
resemblance to those moments in any
long estrangement when—yes—even

you've been known to forget, almost,
how the end got started. Very briefly,
the forgetting stands—seems to—for late

affection, falling with all the casualness of
snow at first, of ruin in a land that was once
called Ruin as, imperceptibly, the curtain lifted.

Riding Westward

Any sunset, look at him: standing there,
like between his legs there's a horse
somehow, on either side of it a saddlebag
of loss, a pack of sorrow, and him Kid
Compromise his very own shoot-'em-up,
tilt-to-the-brim-of-his-hat self, smirk to match,
all-for-love-if-it's-gotta-come-to-that half
swagger,
        half unintentional, I think, sashay.
The silver spurs at his ankles where maybe
the wings would be, if the gods still existed,
catch the light, lose it, as he stands in place,
scraping the dirt with his boots: lines, circles
that stop short, shapes that mean nothing—
no bull, not like that, but scraping shyly, like
a man who's forgotten that part of himself,
keeps forgetting, because what the fuck?

As he takes his hat off; as he lifts his head
like if right now he could be any animal he'd
choose coyote; as all the usual sunset colors
break over his face,
        he starts up singing again,
same as every night, same song: loneliness
by starlight, miles to go, lay me down by
the cool, etc.—that kind of song, the kind
you'll have heard before, sure, somewhere,

but where *was* that,
                        the singer turning this
and that way, as if watching the song itself
—the words to the song—leave him, as he
lets each go, the wind carrying most of it,
some of the words, falling, settling into
instead that larger darkness, where the smaller

darknesses that our lives were lie softly down.